OLD KING COLE'S
BOOK OF NURSERY RHYMES

illustrated by Byam Shaw

being a facsimile edition

Facsimile Classics Series

THE ROMANCE OF
    KING ARTHUR
    by Alfred W. Pollard abridged
    from Malory
    illustrated by Arthur Rackham
IRISH FAIRY TALES
    by James Stephens
    illustrated by Arthur Rackham
THE MIKADO
    by Sir W. S. Gilbert
    illustrated by W. Russell Flint and
    Charles E. Brock
THE YEOMEN OF THE GUARD
    by Sir W. S. Gilbert
    illustrated by W. Russell Flint and
    Charles E. Brock
THE FABLES OF AESOP
    edited by Joseph Jacobs
    illustrated by Richard Heighway
THE WATER-BABIES
    by Charles Kingsley
    illustrated by Linley Sambourne and
    J. MacFarlane
TOM BROWN'S SCHOOLDAYS
    by Thomas Hughes
    illustrated by Arthur Hughes and
    Sydney Prior Hall
ENGLISH FAIRY TALES
    by Flora Annie Steel
    illustrated by Arthur Rackham
THE HEROES OF ASGARD
    by A. and E. Keary
    illustrated by Charles E. Brock
OLD CHRISTMAS
    by Washington Irving
    illustrated by Randolph Caldecott
GRIMM'S HOUSEHOLD
    STORIES
    translated by Lucy Crane
    illustrated by Walter Crane
THE FAIRY BOOK
    by Dinah Maria Mulock
    illustrated by Warwick Goble
JAPANESE FAIRY TALES
    by Grace James
    illustrated by Warwick Goble

THE NURSERY 'ALICE'
    by Lewis Carroll
    illustrated by Sir John Tenniel
THE CUCKOO CLOCK
    by Mary Louisa Molesworth
    illustrated by Charles E. Brock
THE STORY OF SYLVIE
    AND BRUNO
    by Lewis Carroll
    illustrated by Harry Furniss
GULLIVER'S TRAVELS
    by Jonathan Swift
    illustrated by Charles E. Brock
THE HEROES
    by Charles Kingsley
    illustrated by H. M. Brock
RIP VAN WINKLE and
    THE LEGEND OF SLEEPY
    HOLLOW
    by Washington Irving
    illustrated by George H. Boughton
JUST SO STORIES
    by Rudyard Kipling
    illustrated by the author and
    Joseph M. Gleeson
THE MAGIC CITY
    by E. Nesbit
    illustrated by H. R. Millar
THE MAGIC WORLD
    by E. Nesbit
    illustrated by H. R. Millar and
    Spencer Pryse
THE NIGHT BEFORE
    CHRISTMAS
    by Clement C. Moore
    illustrated by W. W. Denslow
OLD KING COLE'S BOOK OF
    NURSERY RHYMES
    illustrated by Byam Shaw
TWO YEARS BEFORE
    THE MAST
    by Richard Henry Dana, Jr
    illustrated by Charles Pears
THE CROCK OF GOLD
    by James Stephens
    illustrated by Thomas MacKenzie

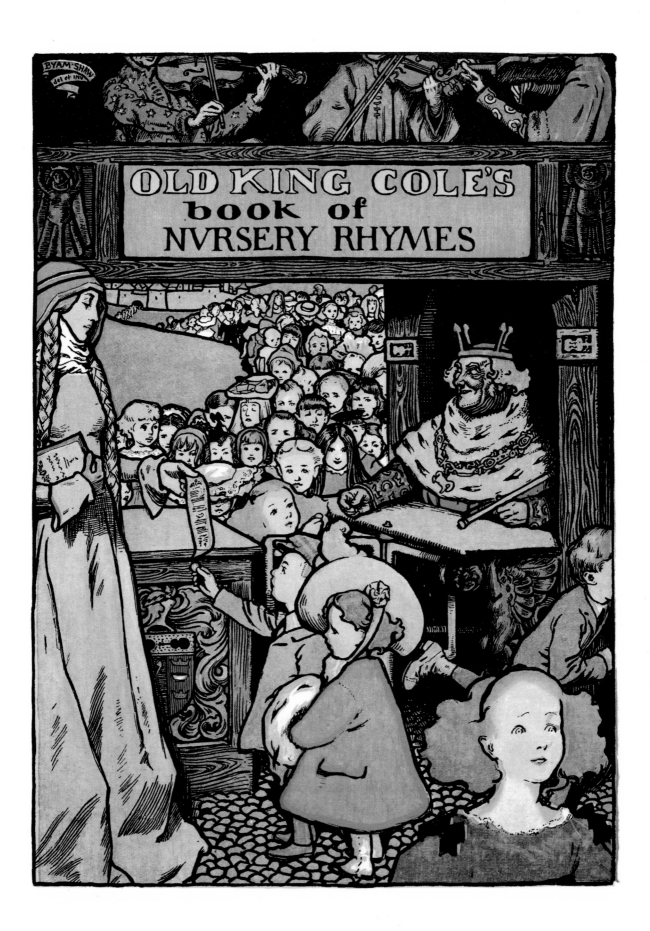

First published by Macmillan & Co. 1901
First published in this edition 1980 by
MACMILLAN PUBLISHERS LTD
4 Little Essex Street London WC2R 3LF

All rights reserved

ISBN: 0 333 30784 4

Printed in Hong Kong

OLD KING COLE

OLD King Cole
Was a merry old soul,
And a merry old soul was he.
He called for his pipe,
And he called for his bowl,
And he called for his fiddlers three.
Every fiddler, he had a fiddle,
And a very fine fiddle had he,
Twee-tweedle-dee, tweedle-dee, went the fiddlers.
Oh, there's none so rare
As can compare
With King Cole and his fiddlers three.

I HAD A LITTLE HUSBAND

I HAD a little husband, no bigger than my
thumb;
I put him in a pint pot, and there I bid him drum.
I bought a little horse, that galloped up and down;
I bridled him, and saddled him, and sent him out
of town.
I gave him some garters, to garter up his hose;
And a little handkerchief, to wipe his pretty nose.

BYAM·SHAW

I HAD A LITTLE HVSBAND NO BIGGER THAN MY THVMB

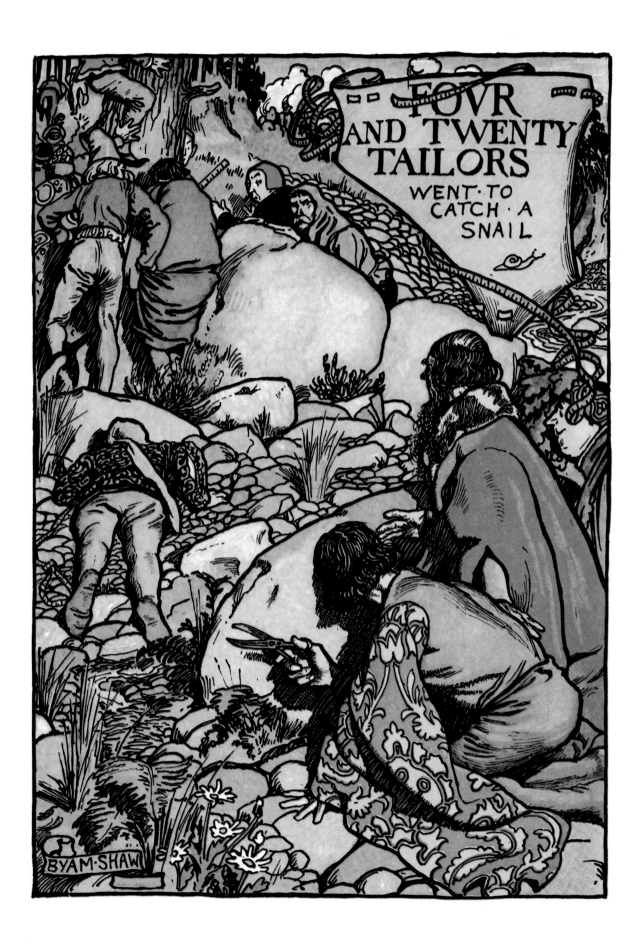

FOVR AND TWENTY TAILORS WENT·TO CATCH·A SNAIL

BYAM·SHAW

FOUR=AND=TWENTY TAILORS

FOUR-AND-TWENTY tailors went to catch a snail,
The best man amongst them durst not touch her tail;
She put out her horns, like a little Kyloe cow,
Run, tailors, run, or she'll kill you all just now.

SNEEZE ON MONDAY

IF you sneeze on Monday, you sneeze for
    danger;
Sneeze on a Tuesday, kiss a stranger;
Sneeze on a Wednesday, sneeze for a letter;
Sneeze on a Thursday, something better;
Sneeze on a Friday, sneeze for sorrow;
Sneeze on a Saturday, see your sweetheart to-morrow.

LADY
DD QVEEN
ANNE
SHE·SITS
IN·THE
SVN

BYAM·SHAW

LADY QUEEN ANNE

QUEEN ANNE, Queen Anne, she sits in the
    sun,
As fair as the lily, as white as the swan:
I send you three letters, so pray you read one.
I cannot read one unless I read all;
So pray, Master Teddy, deliver the ball.

THERE WAS AN OLD WOMAN

THERE was an old woman who rode on a broom,
  With a high gee ho, gee humble;
And she took her old cat behind for a groom,
  With a bimble, bamble, bumble.

They travell'd along till they came to the sky,
  With a high gee ho, gee humble;
But the journey so long made them very hungry,
  With a bimble, bamble, bumble.

Says Tom, I can find nothing here to eat,
  With a high gee ho, gee humble;
So let us go back again, I entreat,
  With a bimble, bamble, bumble.

The old woman would not go back so soon,
  With a high gee ho, gee humble;
For she wanted to visit the Man in the Moon,
  With a bimble, bamble, bumble.

Says Tom, I'll go back by myself to our house,
  With a high gee ho, gee humble;
For there I can catch a good rat or a mouse,
  With a bimble, bamble, bumble.

But, says the old woman, how will you go?
  With a high gee ho, gee humble;
You shan't have my nag, I protest and vow,
  With a bimble, bamble, bumble.

No, no, says Tom, I've a plan of my own,
  With a high gee ho, gee humble;
So he slid down the rainbow, and left her alone,
  With a bimble, bamble, bumble.

A WAS AN ARCHER

A was an Archer, who shot at a frog,
B was a Butcher, who kept a bull-dog.
C was a Captain, all covered with lace,
D was a Drummer, who played with much grace.
E was an Esquire, with pride on his brow,
F was a Farmer, who followed the plough.
G was a Gamester, who had but ill luck,
H was a Hunter, who hunted a buck.
I was an Italian, who had a white mouse,
J was a Joiner, who built up a house.
K was a King, so mighty and grand,
L was a Lady, who had a white hand.
M was a Miser, who hoarded up gold,
N was a Nobleman, gallant and bold.
O was an Organ boy, who played about town,
P was a Parson, who wore a black gown.
Q was a Queen, who was fond of her people,
R was a Robin, who perched on a steeple.
S was a Sailor, who spent all he got,
T was a Tinker, who mended a pot.
U was an Usher, who loved little boys,
V was a Veteran, who sold pretty toys.
W was a Watchman who guarded the door,
X was expensive, and so became poor.
Y was a Youth, who did not love school,
Z was a Zany, who looked a great fool.

COME TO BED, SAYS SLEEPY HEAD

COME, let's to bed, says Sleepy Head,

Tarry a while, says Slow;

Put on the pan, says Greedy Nan,

Let's sup before we go.

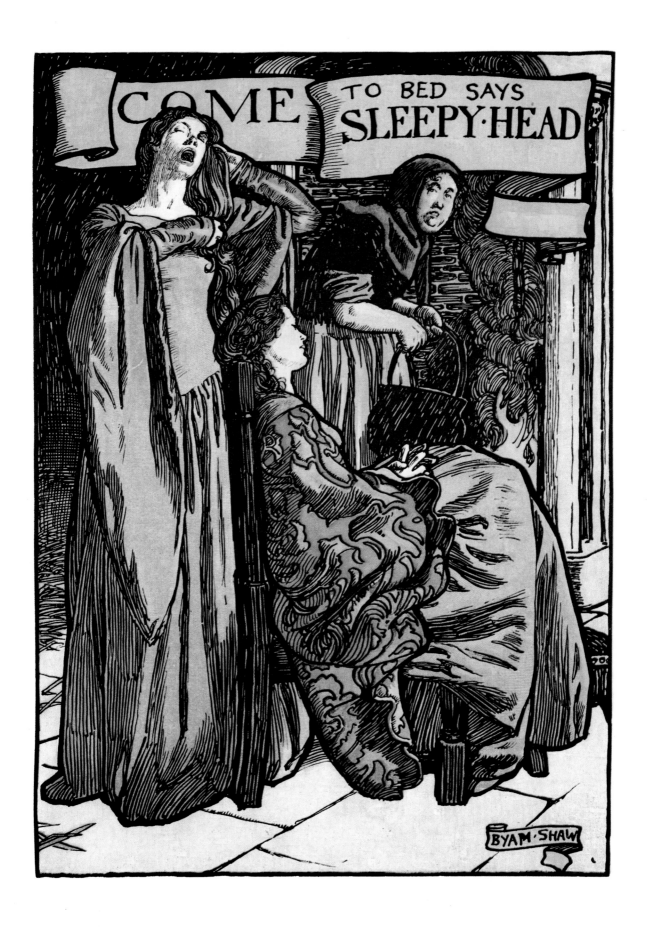

THIS LITTLE PIG WENT
TO MARKET

A Song set to five fingers or toes.

THIS little pig went to market;

This little pig stayed at home;

This little pig eat roast beef;

This little pig had none;

This little pig cried, "Wee, wee, wee!

I can't find my way home!"

LITTLE POLLY FLINDERS

LITTLE Polly Flinders
Sat among the cinders
Warming her pretty little toes.
Her mother came and caught her,
And smacked her little daughter
For spoiling her nice new clothes.

LITTLE POLLY FLINDERS

SAT AMONG THE CINDERS

BARBER, BARBER, SHAVE A PIG

BARBER, barber, shave a pig,
How many hairs will make a wig?
"Four-and-twenty, that's enough."
Give the barber a pinch of snuff.

THE LION AND THE UNICORN

THE Lion and the Unicorn,
　　Fighting for the Crown;
The Lion beat the Unicorn
All round the town.
Some gave them white bread,
Some gave them brown;
Some gave them plum-cake,
And sent them out of town.

THE LION & THE VNICORN
FIGHTING FOR
THE CROWN

BYAM·SHAW
del et inv

LITTLE BO-PEEP

HAS LOST HER SHEEP

BYAM·SHAW

LITTLE BO=PEEP

LITTLE Bo-Peep, she lost her sheep,
  And didn't know where to find them;
Let them alone, they'll all come home
  And bring their tails behind them.

Little Bo-Peep fell fast asleep,
  And dreamt she heard them bleating;
But when she awoke, she found it a joke,
  For they were still a-fleeting.

Then up she took her little crook,
  Determined for to find them;
She found them indeed, but it made her heart bleed,
  For they'd left their tails behind them.

It happened one day, as Bo-Peep did stray
  Into a meadow hard by,
There she espied their tails side by side,
  All hung on a tree to dry.

She heaved a sigh and wiped her eye,
  Then went o'er hill and dale,
And tried what she could, as a shepherdess should,
  To tack to each sheep its tail.

IF ALL THE WORLD WERE WATER

IF all the world were water,
  And all the water were ink,
What should we do for bread and cheese?
What should we do for drink?

GOOSEY GOOSEY GANDER

BYAM·SHAW

STAIRS· & ·DOWNSTAIRS· & ·IN·MY·LADY'S·CHAMBER

GOOSEY, GOOSEY, GANDER

GOOSEY, goosey, gander,
   Where shall I wander?
Up stairs, down stairs,
   And in my lady's chamber;
There I met an old man
   That would not say his prayers;
I took him by the left leg,
   And threw him down stairs.

ROCK=A=BYE, BABY, ON THE TREE TOP

ROCK-A-BYE, baby, on the tree top,
    When the wind blows the cradle will rock,
When the wind lulls, the cradle will fall,
Down will come baby and cradle and all.

ROCK-A-BYE BABY ON THE TREE TOP

WHEN THE WIND BLOWS THE CRADLE WILL ROCK

BYAM-SHAW dd 4

PETER PIPER PICKED·A·PECK OF·PICKLED·PEPPER

BY·A·M·SHAW

PETER PIPER

PETER PIPER picked a peck of pickled
pepper;
A peck of pickled pepper Peter Piper picked;
If Peter Piper picked a peck of pickled pepper,
Where's the peck of pickled pepper Peter
Piper picked?

HERE GOES MY LORD

HERE goes my lord
    A trot, a trot, a trot, a trot;
Here goes my lady
A canter, a canter, a canter, a canter!
Here goes my young master
Jockey-hitch, Jockey-hitch, Jockey-hitch,
    Jockey-hitch;
Here goes my young miss,
An amble, an amble, an amble, an amble!

HERE · GOES ·
MY · LORD

A · TROT · A · TROT
A · TROT · A · TROT

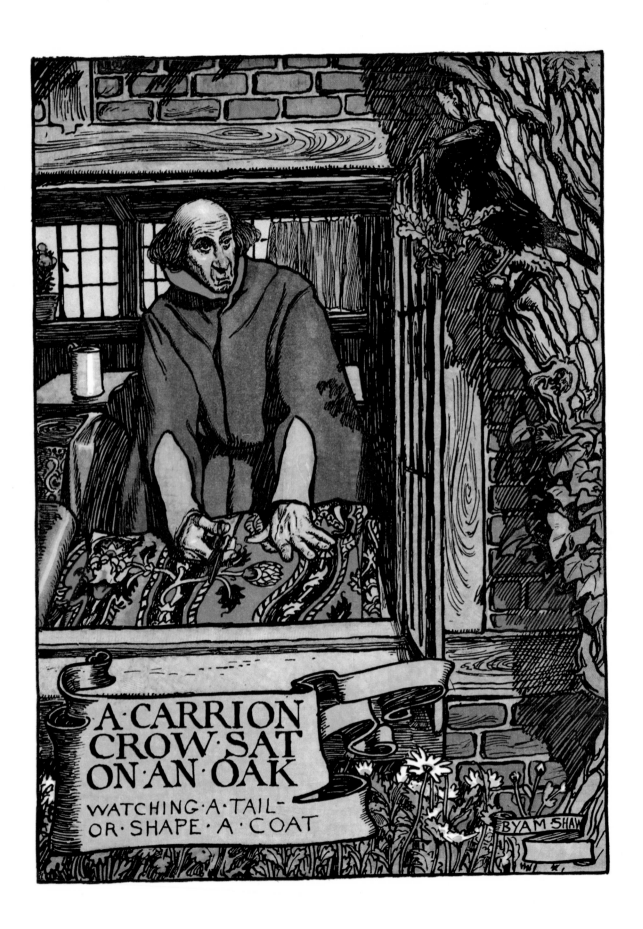

A·CARRION
CROW·SAT
ON·AN·OAK
WATCHING·A·TAIL-
OR·SHAPE·A·COAT

BYAM SHAW

A CARRION CROW SAT ON AN OAK

A CARRION CROW sat on an oak,
  Derry, derry, derry, decco;
A carrion crow sat on an oak,
Watching a tailor shape a coat.
  Heigh-ho! the carrion crow,
  Derry, derry, derry, decco.

"O wife, bring me my old bent bow,"
  Derry, derry, derry, decco;
"O wife, bring me my old bent bow,
"That I may shoot yon carrion crow."
  Heigh-ho! the carrion crow,
  Derry, derry, derry, decco.

The tailor shot, and he missed his mark,
  Derry, derry, derry, decco;
The tailor shot, and he missed his mark,
And shot his old sow right through the heart.
  Heigh-ho! the carrion crow,
  Derry, derry, derry, decco.

"O wife, bring brandy in a spoon,"
  Derry, derry, derry, decco;
"O wife, bring brandy in a spoon,
"For our old sow is in a swoon."
  Heigh-ho! the carrion crow,
  Derry, derry, derry, decco.

THREE WISE MEN OF GOTHAM

THREE wise men of Gotham
Went to sea in a bowl:
If the bowl had been stronger,
My song had been longer.

THREE·WISE
MEN OF GOTHAM

LITTLE MISS MUFFET

LITTLE Miss Muffet,
   She sat on a tuffet,
Eating of curds and whey;
   There came a great spider,
   Who sat down beside her,
And frightened Miss Muffet away.

SIMPLE SIMON

SIMPLE SIMON met a pieman,
    Going to the fair:
Says Simple Simon to the pieman,
    "Let me taste your ware."

Says the pieman to Simple Simon,
    "Show me first your penny."
Says Simple Simon to the pieman,
    "Indeed I have not any."

Simple Simon went a-fishing
    For to catch a whale;
All the water he had got
    Was in his mother's pail.

Simple Simon went to look
    If plums grew on a thistle;
He pricked his fingers very much,
    Which made poor Simon whistle.

SIMPLE SIMON MET A PIE-MAN

GOING·TO·THE·FAIR

BY A.M. SHAW

I·SAW· THREE SHIPS A-SAILING
BY

BYAM·SHAW

I SAW THREE SHIPS

I SAW three ships come sailing by,
  come sailing by, come sailing by—
I saw three ships come sailing by,
 New Year's Day in the morning.

And what do you think was in them then,
  was in them then, was in them then?
And what do you think was in them then?
 New Year's Day in the morning

Three pretty girls were in them then,
  were in them then, were in them then—
Three pretty girls were in them then,
 New Year's Day in the morning.

One could whistle and another could sing,
  and the other could play on the violin—
Such joy was there at my wedding,
 New Year's Day in the morning.

THREE BLIND MICE

THREE blind mice,
    See how they run!
They all ran after the farmer's wife,
Who cut off their tails with a carving knife.
Did you ever see such a thing in your life
    As three blind mice?

THREE
BLIND
MICE

BYAM·SHAW